GW00302381

First published in Great Britain 2023 by Farshore
An imprint of HarperCollins*Publishers*
1 London Bridge Street, London SE1 9GF
www.farshore.co.uk

HarperCollins*Publishers*
Macken House,
39/40 Mayor Street Upper,
Dublin 1
D01 C9W8

Special thanks to Sherin Kwan, Alex Wiltshire, Jay Castello, Milo Bengtsson,
Craig Leigh, Dennis Ries, Nathan Rose, Kelsey Ranallo and Kevin Grace.

ISBN 978 0 0085 9501 2
Printed in Italy
1

ONLINE SAFETY FOR YOUNGER FANS

Spending time online is great fun! Here are a few simple rules to help younger fans stay safe and
keep the internet a great place to spend time:
- Never give out your real name – don't use it as your username.
- Never give out any of your personal details.
- Never tell anybody which school you go to or how old you are.
- Never tell anybody your password except a parent or a guardian.
- Be aware that you must be 13 or over to create an account on many sites.
Always check the site policy and ask a parent or guardian for permission before registering.
- Always tell a parent or guardian if something is worrying you.
Stay safe online. Any website addresses listed in this book are correct at the time of going to print.
However, Farshore is not responsible for content hosted by third parties. Please be aware that online
content can be subject to change and websites can contain content that is unsuitable for children.
We advise that all children are supervised when using the internet.

Stay safe online. Farshore is not responsible for content hosted by third parties.

CONTENTS

HELLO

Hello, and welcome to the world of Minecraft Legends! You're just in time: those piglins are about to cause some real trouble. From the very first day of work on Legends, the teams at Mojang and Blackbird Interactive wanted to create a new kind of strategy game for players like you and we hope that you're both challenged and delighted by the adventure to come.

- MOJANG STUDIOS

THE OVERWORLD NEEDS A HERO

SOME LEGENDS TELL OF PEACE. SOME TELL OF DANGER AND THE END OF ALL THINGS.

In Minecraft Legends, you'll explore a familiar yet mysterious land, full of diverse life, lush biomes and a widespread abundance of resources. But this paradise is on the brink of destruction. The piglins have arrived, hungry to take the Overworld for themselves.

Learn how to take the fight to the piglins before their Nether corruption engulfs the entire Overworld! Discover how to inspire unexpected friends and lead them into battle, while making the most of the Overworld's rich resources. Gather materials, build structures, unlock upgrades and learn strategies to stay one step ahead of the marauding piglins.

THIS IS THE LEGEND OF A UNITED OVERWORLD.

UNITED ... BY YOU.

WELCOME, HERO

COMMANDING YOUR ALLIES

The piglins' invasion will test the abilities of any player. Successfully defending the Overworld will require the use of strategies, such as directing your allies, using your resources and choosing the right time to charge in to battle. Can you lead with your mind as well as your might?

TOTAL CONTROL

To have the best view of all the action, you will need to use the third-person camera to your advantage. Keep a close eye on every part of the battlefield, so you can react and adapt your tactics to the ever-changing action around you.

OPEN WORLD

The Overworld is a big place with lots of different biomes and inhabitants. The more time you spend exploring the biomes, the faster you'll identify the benefits and dangers of each one.

THE HOSTS

Your adventure begins when you are recruited by the three caretakers of the Overworld, known as the Hosts. They will tell you about the invasion and guide you through your adventure.

ACTION

Action is the most outspoken Host and often speaks of their care and love for all beings of the Overworld. Softly spoken and young at heart, Action can sometimes be impatient and show emotion before the other Hosts.

FORESIGHT

The wisest of the Hosts, Foresight has insight into what might come to pass. They always see several possibilities, and can't be sure which one will happen. Because of this, they are cautious and will always give much thought before taking decisive action.

KNOWLEDGE

Small in size but immeasurable in intelligence, Knowledge created the powerful tools you have at your disposal – the Legendary Lute, the Banner of Command and the Lantern of Creation. Knowledge believes that mastering these tools will be the key to saving the Overworld.

PLAY MODES

There is more than one way to jump into the action in Minecraft Legends. You can choose to play the campaign alone or cooperatively with a friend, or you can rush head first into online PVP battles.

CAMPAIGN

Your journey starts just after the piglin invasion has begun. Their attacks will show up on your map and you must race to defeat their hordes. Be warned – they won't give up. Their nightly invasions will grow more ferocious and their bases will expand. Your determination alone won't be enough, so you'll have to upgrade your abilities and call on mobs to join the fight to save the Overworld.

PVP MODE

The Player Vs Player mode lets you pit your wits and test your tactics against other players from around the world. Jump straight into the action as part of a team and dominate fast and furious battle rounds in head-to-head combat.

COOPERATIVE PLAY

Connect with other players with cross-platform cooperative play. Join a raging battle just as it needs your help, or allow new recruits into your game the second all hope looks lost. You can play the whole campaign with up to three other players!

THE GAME SCREEN

1. COMPASS
Follow the beacons to travel to villages under attack or locate piglin bases.

2. RESOURCES
See the amount of each resource you've collected and have available to use.

3. ALLAY COMMANDS
Use this menu to command your allays to gather resources, or to build spawners, structures and upgrades.

4. TASK HOTBAR
Depending on which allay command you've selected, this hotbar will show your available options for each category.

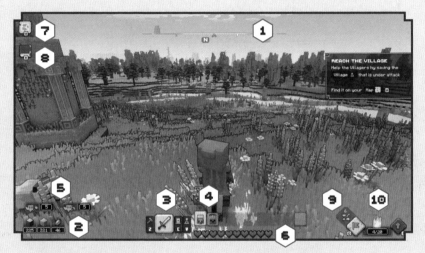

5. ALLAYS
Displays the number of allays you have to gather valuable resources or build structures.

6. HEALTH BAR
This displays your current health status. If it drops too low, take a break from battle.

7. OVERWORLD MAP
Press the button shown here to open your map. Use this to fast travel and to see what the piglins are planning.

8. SONGBOOK
Your songbook documents all the Lute tunes you can play to command your allays, and lets you customise your task hotbars.

9. LURED UNITS
When you are commanding your allies, this will show you how many units you currently have lured, and at your command.

10. QUICK COMMANDS
Select your sword or the Banner of Command here. The flame icon shows how many allies you can have in your army.

HERO SELECT

You may be just beginning your life as a hero, but you could become the most famous face in the Overworld. It's important to look the part! The Hero Select screen is your first chance to express yourself.

CHOOSE YOUR CHARACTER

There are five unique and exciting heroes to choose from when you start the campaign. Your choice will not have an effect on your armour or abilities, but wouldn't it be pretty cool to save the day in your favourite style?

CHAMPION

Strike fear into the hearts of all piglins with this champion's outfit.

GUARDIAN

A guardian is dressed to defend the Overworld from any enemies.

MAGUS

Wear this regal look if you really want to rule over the battlefield.

ADVENTURER

A true adventurer wants nothing more than to battle piglins!

RANGER

A hood adds an element of mystery to this explorer look.

EXTRA OPTIONS

There are several additional options available to heroes. If you would like to try something brand-new, you can access the Minecraft Legends marketplace and download exciting new skins. You can even wear your favourite styles from the Minecraft Dressing Room.

YOUR TRUSTED MOUNT

Every hero needs a trusty steed to navigate the Overworld. Once you have found a mount in the wild, it will wait for you at village fountains.

HORSE

Fast and dependable, the horse mount will never shy away from battle. It is extremely confident crossing all types of terrain, from plains to mountains.

BIG BEAK

This winged wonder has the highest leap and can glide long distances. Perfect for travelling over mountains and valleys.

REGAL TIGER

This purple tiger is perfect for chasing down piglins. It is the fastest of the mounts and can cover ground in no time, but can't jump as well as the others.

BRILLIANT BEETLE

The beetle is loyal, dependable and has the unique ability to climb walls and float in the breeze. It is the quickest mount for crossing water.

A HERO'S TOOLS

As a new hero, you will need to master the tools you have at your disposal. Each one was carefully crafted by the Host of Knowledge and will help you boss epic battles, command your allies and build structures that will enable you to defend villages and attack bases.

SWORD

The first tool you will wield is your sword. You can charge into battle and swing your blade to take out basic piglin units, but advanced piglins will take longer to defeat.

LEGENDARY LUTE

An elegant instrument that fills the world with music and magic. The melodies it creates will delight and inspire your allays, and are your way of communicating with them when you need to gather resources or build vital structures.

ALLAYS

These colourful mobs are mysterious and will only communicate using music. Blue allays will gather resources for you, while yellow ones will build structures and upgrades. Allays have a strong link with the Hosts, and they are looking forward to getting to know you.

FLAME OF CREATION

The special case that holds the flame will allow you to summon powerful allies. They will fight by your side as long as the flame continues to burn.

You can upgrade and increase your allays at the Well of Fate. This enables you to gather more resources and build more structures at the same time.

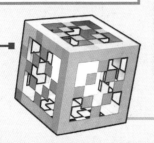

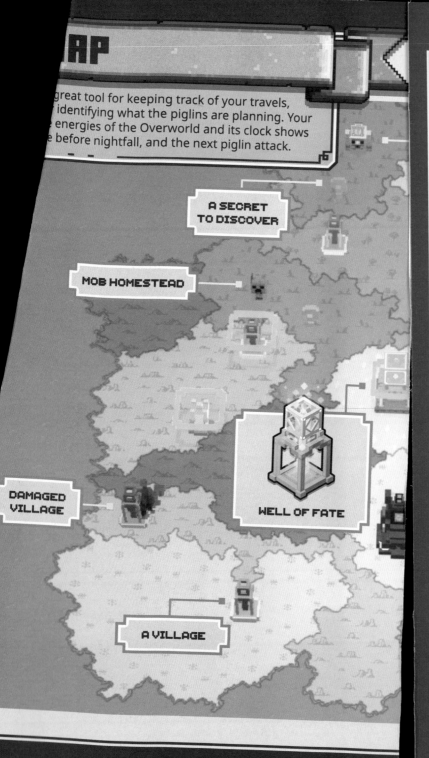

...AP

...great tool for keeping track of your travels, ...identifying what the piglins are planning. Your ...energies of the Overworld and its clock shows ...e before nightfall, and the next piglin attack.

A SECRET TO DISCOVER

MOB HOMESTEAD

DAMAGED VILLAGE

WELL OF FATE

A VILLAGE

BANNER OF COMMAND

The Banner of Command is only as powerful as the person holding it. In your hands, it will become a symbol of hope and unity across the Overworld, and an essential tool to command your allies and drive the piglins back to the Nether.

GATHER

If you're outnumbered and in a bind, then hold the Banner of Command above your head. All allies within close range of you will be commanded to come to your side and stay close by.

DIRECT

You can use the Banner of Command to send your lured allies in whichever way you're facing. They will charge in that direction and attack the first enemies or structure they meet.

TARGET TACTICALLY

In Banner View, you can give very specific orders to the right number and types of your allies. This enables you to send a mob or group of mobs to a specific target and nothing will distract them until they get there. You can direct specific mobs for certain jobs, such as sending creepers to cause explosive damage to structures.

Your health will take damage if you get too close to some piglin structures, such as blaze rod towers. Use the Banner of Command to send a group of cobblestone golems to destroy them, while you remain at a safe distance.

GAME K

Your in-game map is a
but it is most useful fo
map is in tune with the
you how long you hav

THE OVE

From grassy plains to sn
mountains, the Overwor
biomes, and every new g
a unique world to discover. You
mobs, valuable resources and m
structures that connect everythi

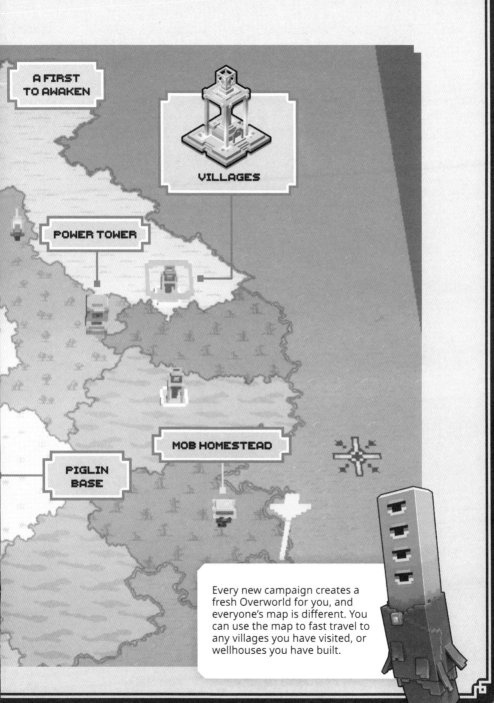

A FIRST TO AWAKEN

VILLAGES

POWER TOWER

MOB HOMESTEAD

PIGLIN BASE

Every new campaign creates a fresh Overworld for you, and everyone's map is different. You can use the map to fast travel to any villages you have visited, or wellhouses you have built.

OVERWORLD BIOMES

The more you get to know the different biomes, the easier you will find it to navigate between them and make the most of the resources they offer. Let's take a closer look at what you can expect to find.

FATELANDS

The fatelands are home to many peaceful mobs, but are best known for rolling green hills, rock formations and colourful wildflowers – not to mention iron and cobblestone to gather. You will spend lots of time at the Well of Fate, building upgrades for your abilities.

TUNDRA

The tundra is so bitterly cold, it is quite amazing that skeletons have their homestead here. There are large, sweeping waves of ice and sunken hot springs that can randomly erupt and launch you high into the sky. Look for rare diamond ore sparkling here.

SWAMP

This lush swampland is packed with tall trees and mangroves, and is the ideal home for mobs that enjoy mud puddles. Thick redthorn bushes might cause you some minor damage, but there is plenty of redstone to gather here, which makes it worth a visit.

DRY SAVANNA

An arid landscape of dried grass and stone outcrops, you'd be forgiven for thinking life would be a struggle in this savanna. Explore here if you need to gather valuable iron ore, but don't leave until you witness its intriguing watering holes and gather any iron you find.

JUNGLE

Thick forests of high-canopied trees and dangerously long venom vines make the jungle an easy place to get lost. Look for strange glowing mushrooms if you need to jump away from danger ... but not before you've gathered some useful redstone ore.

FOREST

If you notice the foliage change colour on your travels, there's a chance you've wandered into the forest. This tree-filled territory is full of scurrying creatures who call it home. Winding streams cut through the trees and there's iron you can gather, but be on the lookout for mud puddles that will slow you down.

MEADOW

The vast open plains of the meadow biome are populated with low-lying hills and snaking rivers. If you walk the riverbanks, you'll discover playful mobs enjoying the peace. There's an abundance of coal, so don't forget to call on your own playful allays to gather it for you before you move on.

BADLANDS

The badlands are dominated by prehistoric-looking plateaus with sticky tar pits and steep buttes. It may look inhospitable, but hidden in the shadows of its deep valleys are vibrant plant life and plentiful amounts of coal to gather.

JAGGED PEAKS

If you see huge mountains that tower into the clouds, then you're near the jagged peaks. The falls are steep and deep, so if you're scared of heights, don't look down – even if you spot precious diamond ore. The right mount is essential when you travel here.

The Overworld is surrounded by a vast ocean. While you can swim, little is known of this mysterious area and exploring it will offer you no rewards.

THE WELL OF FATE

You will discover many interesting locations across the Overworld, but none as important as the Well of Fate. Nestled among the rolling hills and rocky outcrops of the fatelands, this impressive structure is an icon of unity, and vital to your mission.

THE HOSTS

This location is a shining light that ties the Overworld together and is connected to every corner of the land. Every time you return here, you'll find the Hosts going about their business and you can use your resources to build upgraded structures.

SYMBOL

The Well of Fate is the origin of all life in the Overworld and stands tall as a beacon of unity, renewal and harmony. Unsurprisingly, it is the piglin's top target. If the Well of Fate falls, the whole of the Overworld will follow.

CONNECTED

The water from the well's spring travels all across the Overworld. It flows from all functioning fountains in every village, so you can fast-travel to any flowing village fountain and any wellhouse you have built.

UPGRADES

The Well of Fate is where you can improve your abilities and upgrade structures. The more experience you gain, the more improvements you can make. Let's look at how you can change your game!

ABUNDANT ALLAYS

This improvement increases the number of allays at your command, allowing you to build more structures and gather extra resources. Each additional improvement will add build allays and gather allays to your team.

REQUIRED

ALLAY STORAGE

This valuable upgrade builds a fate bank, which enables you to carry more resources and keep them stored safely until you need them. Each time you build an improvement, you can store more wood, stone, lapis, prismarine and gold.

REQUIRED

IMPROVEMENT: BANNER

Rallying mobs is one of the first skills you will learn, but upgrading your Banner of Command allows you to rally more friends to follow you into battle. Each additional improvement enables more mobs to rally around you at once.

REQUIRED

FLAMES OF CREATION

This upgrades your Flames so that you may spawn more mobs at any time and have a larger army of allies. You can use this upgrade twice, but it is with the second use that you will see a larger and more effective change to your abilities.

REQUIRED

GATHER IRON

One of the first available upgrades will inspire your allays to gather iron. This key resource is used to build grindstone and mossy golems, masonry huts and wellhouses. Each improvement allows you to carry additional iron.

REQUIRED

GATHER REDSTONE

Redstone is used to spawn zombies and is a core crafting component. It's a vital ingredient in mechanical contraptions, such as the battle drum and redstone launcher. This upgrade allows you to gather extra redstone every time you build it.

REQUIRED

GATHER COAL

This enables you to gather coal, which is used to spawn creepers and build new structures, such as the kaboomery, scatter towers and protector towers. It allows chests in the meadow biome to contain coal, and each improvement allows you to carry more coal.

REQUIRED

GATHER DIAMOND

Discover the power of diamonds with this dazzling melody. It will enable your allays to gather diamond, which you will need to spawn skeletons. Diamond can also be used to build useful structures, such as spyglasses and freeze traps.

REQUIRED

CURE NETHERRACK

Piglins contaminate ground with netherrack, which prevents you building. This will cure the land.

REQUIRED

GATHER ALL

After building all gather upgrades, you will be gifted this melody to gather all resources within range.

REQUIRED

COMPLETE ALL GATHER UPGRADES

WAKE THE FIRSTS

You may discover the Firsts, but you need this upgrade to be able to awaken them and use resources to rebuild them.

REQUIRED

SHARED VILLAGE CHESTS

This connects all village chests together, so you can collect resources from every chest at once.

REQUIRED

EXPERT CARPENTRY

Only available to use once, this upgrade increases carpenter hut repair speeds and construction speeds.

REQUIRED

EXPERT MASON

This helps convert your structures to stone faster and increases your masonry hut's effective range.

REQUIRED

COLLECT POWER TOWERS

This improvement is needed to collect and rebuild any power towers you find on your travels.

REQUIRED

MOB HOMESTEADS

You will encounter familiar mobs roaming all across the Overworld but each one has its own homestead – a place to live, a place to feel safe and a place to call home. As your legend grows, the mobs will choose to fight alongside you, as long as you keep their homesteads safe ...

CREEPER HOMESTEAD

The most reclusive of mobs, you'll do well to locate these creeper grounds. This collection of stone and sulphur buildings is found in the vast barrens of the badlands. While the glowing green springs are an intriguing sight, this area is low in resources and often surrounded by an abundance of redthorn bushes, so approach with caution.

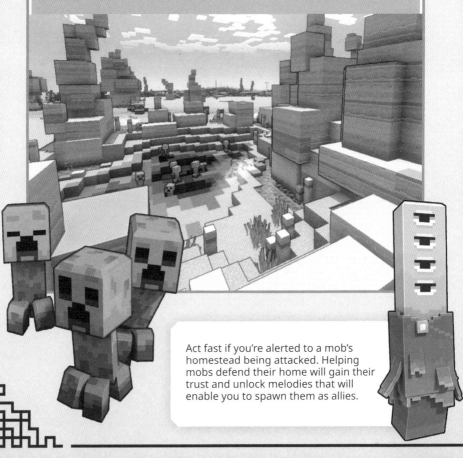

Act fast if you're alerted to a mob's homestead being attacked. Helping mobs defend their home will gain their trust and unlock melodies that will enable you to spawn them as allies.

SKELETON HOMESTEAD

Home to the chattering bones of the skeletons. At its centre, a fierce skull rises out of the frozen tundra with a hot spring bubbling in its centre. While you won't stumble across many resources in this winter wonderland, rare diamonds can be found if you look closely enough.

ZOMBIE HOMESTEAD

Nestled among the thick trees and blooming corpse flowers of the jungle, you will find the villa that this unassuming bunch call home. Use the glowing bouncecaps to climb to the top of the canopy and you could find allay chests full of rewards, or spot some rare clusters of redstone to gather nearby.

TOWERS

Towers were created by Knowledge and have unique powers. They are scattered far and wide across the Overworld and learning how to use them will be vitally important as you take on increasing piglin numbers.

COLLECT TOWERS

Although you may find towers early in the game, you will not be able to collect them before you build the Collect Power Towers upgrade. This enables you to exchange your valuable gold to collect and keep towers. The more towers you manage to collect, the more you can build on the battlefield.

DISMANTLE AND REBUILD

Once you have unlocked the ability to collect towers, you can choose to use them to gain a tactical advantage in battle. They are particularly effective in protecting villages from the more intense piglin attacks. Once they've done their job, you can dismantle them and rebuild them in different locations.

BLAST TOWER

Capable of delivering epic destructive power, the blast tower can fire projectiles from medium range that will knock back piglins on impact. It is particularly useful when you are battling bigger piglin units, such as brutes and pigmadillos, who require more firepower to slow down and defeat them.

FROST TOWER

The coolest tower of them all! The frost tower can be used to slow down any piglin advances. Aim at groups of powerful troops and it will launch frost cubes that quickly freeze them. This will give you precious time to organise your troops, spawn new allies and start a counter attack.

STUN TOWER

This stunning bell tower emits a powerful sonic wave that will stun any enemies within range, overwhelming them with confusion. It can't cause health damage to its victims, but it will slow enemies down and render them useless until the effects wear off.

RESOURCES

Even the most talented sword swinger will need a helping hand to overpower and outsmart the piglins. Gathering the right resources and learning how to build structures will help you craft a stronger defence of the Overworld.

SO MUCH TO DISCOVER

The Overworld is full of resources and understanding them all will help you in many ways. The better you know them, the more you can utilise mysterious boosts, avoid dangerous hazards and build useful constructions.

BOOSTS

SPEED WHEAT
Found all across the Overworld, speed wheat produces an unstable pollen if you walk through it. This pollen ignites into millions of microscopic explosions, giving you a short burst of extreme speed!

BOUNCECAPS
These brightly coloured mushrooms give off spores that are lighter than air. Touch one and you'll be able to jump to extreme heights and won't take any fall damage – perfect for manoeuvring on mountains!

REGENERATION STONE
These mysterious stones seem as if they have been standing in the Overworld for time beyond knowing. They emit an energy with restorative effects that will regenerate your health.

ALLAY CHESTS
Located randomly around the Overworld, allay chests will routinely build up rewards for your bravery. You may also get lucky and be gifted a new gather allay or build allay to use.

HAZARDS

REDTHORN
Take care as you race across the Overworld on your quest: redthorn grows in patches in many different biomes across the Overworld. Its sharp thorns slow you down and cause you damage.

TAR PIT

These ancient pits might look like treacle, but we highly recommend staying well clear. Get a bit too close and they'll slow you down with their stickiness and make you a static target for attack.

POISON VINE

It's easy to mistake this interesting-looking foliage as harmless, but it is far from it. Come into contact with it and its effects will slowly reduce your health meter.

GEYSER

If you're rushing across the tundra, then you'd be wise to watch your step. There's a good chance you'll walk over a geyser just as it shoots water high into the sky – and you with it!

MUD PUDDLE

The mud puddles you'll encounter were cultivated by dry savannah pigs looking for a way to beat the heat. They don't look very inviting, which is a good thing as they will only serve to slow you down.

RESOURCES

WOOD

A key ingredient in earlier builds, wood is found in almost every biome. It is worth keeping good supplies to build simple walls to protect important structures, such as village fountains.

STONE

Found all across the Overworld, stone is great for building stronger structures with more durability than wood. It is easy to gather and an essential component for many structures and upgrades.

IRON

Iron is a key ingredient when spawning grindstone and mossy golems. It is also used to build wellhouses to expand your fast travel network, and masonry huts, which provide stronger villages.

COAL

Coal is often found in clusters across the meadow and jagged peaks biomes. It can be used to spawn creepers and build advanced structures, such as the kaboomery, which can fire explosive arrows.

REDSTONE

This glowing red resource has the energy to power special structures. If you're placing Host towers, defending with freeze traps or planning to unleash the power of a redstone launcher, then make sure you're fully stocked.

GOLD

Unlike most other resources, gold cannot be gathered by your allays. Instead you can obtain it by destroying piglin portals and gold mines. It is an essential ingredient for building your upgrades at the Well of Fate.

DIAMOND

Hidden in the tundra and jagged peaks, this valuable resource is harder to find than many other resources. It is used to build advanced structures and is a key ingredient in the spawning of skeletons.

LAPIS

This resource cannot be gathered by allays, but you can collect it from village chests and by defeating piglins. It is an important ingredient that you will require when spawning allies at mob spawners.

PRISMARINE

This is a key resource for building improvements and upgrades. It can only be collected by destroying piglin structures. Build upgrades regularly – if you are at your prismarine cap, any newly gathered prismarine will be wasted.

If you're looking for a particular resource, it pays to know where they are most commonly found. Remember what you see in every biome and you'll save yourself time when you need them most.

VILLAGES

These important locations are used as fast travel locations, as long as their fountains are running. Villagers will gather local biome resources in chests for you to collect. The shared village chest upgrade connects all these chests, so you only have to visit one to collect them all.

LOCATIONS

Villages are a key part of the Overworld and can be found across the low-lying biomes. Although you are likely to stumble across them as you explore, they will first be brought to your attention by the Hosts, who will direct you to a desperate village that needs your help.

INHABITANTS

Every village is the home of villagers. These mobs never stray too far into the wilderness and spend their time gathering nearby resources to deposit in the village chest. They will be deeply distressed when their homes are invaded; perhaps you can inspire their bravery?

ATTACKED

While piglins will build their bases everywhere, they know that every village is linked to the Well of Fate, so they're prime targets for destruction. You can choose to actively defend against piglin night attacks, or build defences so the village will protect itself while you are elsewhere.

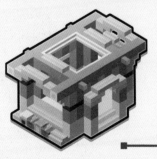

REPAIRS

Defending a village successfully is a heroic moment, but it isn't a time to get complacent. More often than not, the piglins will have caused catastrophic damage. By building a carpenter's hut, you will help the villagers repair their fountain and restore order to their homestead.

VILLAGE DEFENCE

A village that has been targeted for attack will have red arrows around it on your map. You can build defensive structures during the day or actively defend a village against the piglins at night.

PATROL

When a village is attacked, piglins will chase villagers, lock them in cages and cause damage to their structures. If you can eliminate a certain number of piglins, the rest of them will run scared. Swing your sword and drive them out!

BASIC DEFENCE

In the early stages of the game, you can use basic structures to help protect villages. Placing a wooden wall around a fountain will not keep the piglins out forever, but it will slow down their attacks, distract them and buy you time.

ADVANCED

The villagers will benefit from walls protecting their fountain, but it isn't a long-term solution. Once you've upgraded your abilities, you can help villages become stronger than ever with structures, such as arrow towers and blast towers.

The safer villagers feel in their homes, the more resources they'll feel comfortable collecting for the village chest. Build walls and towers to help them feel safe.

FAST TRAVEL NETWORK

From dry savannas to snow-peaked mountain ranges, your journeys between biomes and across the Overworld will take time. If you're in a rush to defend a village or destory a piglin base, you'll need a faster way to travel ...

FOUNTAINS

Using your map, you can return to any village that you have previously visited using fast travel. These have a blue square around them on your map. Select the village you wish to travel to and you and your allies will be transported. If a village is damaged, fast travel is unavailable until the fountain is repaired.

WELLHOUSES

You can create fast travel locations anywhere that you choose by building wellhouses. These could be near piglin bases or areas rich in resources you wish to gather. They also act as respawn points, but be warned, the piglins may target your wellhouses when you aren't looking!

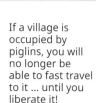

If a village is occupied by piglins, you will no longer be able to fast travel to it ... until you liberate it!

DID YOU KNOW?

You can help keep your wellhouses safe by building walls and arrow towers around their perimeter.

STRUCTURES

Knowing which structures to introduce to your gameplay and when to use them can improve your options in defence and attack. Some offer perfect protection for villages, while others will enable you to access hard-to-reach places and wreak havoc on piglin bases.

WALLS

The wall is a simple but effective method of defence that can be extended around precious structures, such as village fountains or defensive towers. Piglins will try to break down your walls, so keep on top of repairs.

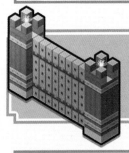

GATES

Using a gate will help strengthen and defend your position. They will automatically open for you and your allies, but slam shut in the face of your enemies, making it harder for them to access villages or your wellhouses.

RAMPS

Some piglin bases will be on higher ground, which makes them difficult to reach for you and your allies. You can use ramps to create stairs or bridges. What's more, they can also be built directly on to netherrack, unlike other structures.

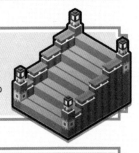

CARPENTER HUT

This is an essential part of repairing villages after they've been attacked. When placing one, it will show a higlighted range – it will repair damaged structures within this influence zone.

IMPROVEMENT:

EXPERT CARPENTRY
This increases the regeneration speed to your structures and makes them more resilient when taking damage.

MASONRY

Build a masonry near your wooden walls, towers and gates, and it permanently turns them from wood into stone. This significantly increases their durability, making them stronger against the piglins' attacks.

IMPROVEMENT:

EXPERT MASON

This one-time improvement adds 100% faster conversion of structures into stone.

ICE TRAP

Placing ice traps as a form of defence will ensure any unwanted visitors receive a frosty reception. Any enemy that walks into the range of an ice trap won't be harmed, but they will be frozen for a limited time.

ARROW TOWERS

These tall towers will shoot arrows at any enemies that stray within its firing range. You can upgrade an arrow tower's effectiveness with a kaboomery, which will make it fire explosive arrows. Any towers within range of a battle drum will have their attack rate increased and a spyglass will greatly increase the arrow tower's range.

UPGRADE WITH:

| KABOOMERY | STONE MASON HUT | BATTLE DRUM | SPYGLASS OVERLOOK |

Combining upgrades can make your builds more powerful in many ways. Turn the page to discover more about each upgrade structure.

SCATTER TOWER

This tower may have a shorter target range than the arrow tower, but it fires at a faster rate and uses more powerful projectiles. You can upgrade its powers by placing other village structures nearby, such as the spyglass overlook.

UPGRADE WITH:

KABOOMERY | STONE MASON HUT | BATTLE DRUM | SPYGLASS OVERLOOK

PROTECTOR TOWER

As the piglins throw more at every battle, their weapons will become more powerful. Combat this with a protector tower, which destroys any large projectiles that they launch in your direction.

UPGRADE WITH:

STONE MASON HUT

REDSTONE LAUNCHER

This advanced launcher is fuelled by the dynamic power of redstone. It must be manually aimed and fired at your targeted area, unlike the arrow and scatter towers. Your reward is a long-range launcher capable of destroying piglin structures.

UPGRADE WITH:

KABOOMERY | BATTLE DRUM | SPYGLASS OVERLOOK

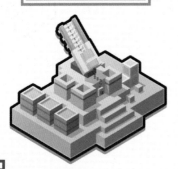

STRUCTURE UPGRADES

There are several options for upgrading your own structures by building additional structures nearby. Here we will look at what each of those are and what changes they will make to your builds.

KABOOMERY

Build a kaboomery near your arrow towers, scatter towers or redstone launchers and it will upgrade them with ... explosive results. It will add a serious knockback to any piglins that wander within range.

BATTLE DRUM

Build a battle drum and you will hear its beat in the heat of combat. It will increase the firing speed of any arrow towers, scatter towers or redstone launchers, and cause problems for the piglins.

SPYGLASS OVERLOOK

A spyglass overlook positioned within the range of your arrow towers, scatter towers or redstone launchers will increase the firing range of their weaponry. Perfect for taking care of piglin units before they get too close.

Before you place a structure, it will highlight an area around its position. This is the area within which its powers will be effective, such as a tower's firing range or a masonry turning structures to stone.

ENEMIES AND ALLIES

Many walks of life have made a home in the Overworld, finding their own space within its numerous biomes. From the living to the undead, they exist harmoniously alongside one another, but the arrival of the piglins threatens to change their homes forever.

THE ENEMY (PIGLINS)

The Overworld has never faced a threat as grotesque as the piglins. Bred in the fiery depths of the Nether, there are three different hordes, each with their own characteristics and tactics, but all with the same goal: to destroy the Overworld's peace and corrupt it with netherrack.

HORDE OF THE BASTION

Size is almost everything to piglins, and the Horde of the Bastion has the biggest piglins and fortifications, so there's no mistaking when you have encountered them. These elite defenders are known for their strength, barbarity and building skills. If they aren't stopped, their huge, high-walled bases will exert a powerful hold over the lands around them.

✦ WHAT TO EXPECT ✦

Thanks to their towers and ranged units, Bastion bases are hard to penetrate. If you destroy their walls or structures, piglins will rush to repair them, and this can often leave you trapped inside and forced into close-quarters combat. Head to page 87 for more tactics on dealing with them.

HORDE OF THE SPORE

The atmosphere changes, your footsteps become muted and the air grows thick with Nether spores. This can mean only one thing ... you're face to face with the Horde of the Spore. This ghastly horde won't rest until they've spread their noxious ways and polluted as much of the Overworld as possible.

✦ WHAT TO EXPECT ✦

They want to spend as much time as possible souring the ground and poisoning the air. Stopping them won't be easy – they build their bases on tall pillars, from which a fall could be fatal. If that wasn't bad enough, they will try to drive you away with waves of ranged lava launcher attacks. Turn to page 89 for more tactics if you're struggling to reach their bases.

You will always be alerted when a new piglin base appears in the world. Catching them early is vitally important.

HORDE OF THE HUNT

This hungry horde is trained to be highly aggressive and totally unforgiving in their tactics. With no walls or gates, their sprawling bases may be easy to enter and navigate, but they are protected with multiple defensive structures close to the portals. If you dare place structures near them, they will send overwhelming numbers of piglins to teach you a lesson.

✛ WHAT TO EXPECT ✛

Your experiences with the other hordes will not be enough to prepare for the Hunt. Their aggression is relentless, and they will stop at nothing just to get to you. Their units will sacrifice themselves and their allies just to slow down your progress. Turn to page 88 for more on battle tactics.

PIGLIN UNITS

Piglins come in lots of shapes and sizes with different strengths and weaknesses. Each horde also has their own unique units! Knowing how to combat each will save you time and prevent extreme losses.

MACE RUNT

The humble mace runt is the lowest form of piglin there is. They lack the brains and brawn to cause you trouble on their own, but they are determined and their strength in numbers is ferocious. In close-quarters situations, they can easily overwhelm you and your allies with random swings of their maces.

STRATEGY TIP

Runts are best approached in two stages: use ranged attacks to thin out their numbers, then charge in with your sword to clean up the rest.

BLAZE RUNT

If a runt survives long enough, they will graduate to the rank of blaze runt. Their mace is replaced with the blaze rod, a fiery projectile that can can cause serious ranged damage. Blaze runts are also better trained than mace runts, and they can use their blaze rods with unrivalled accuracy and aggression.

STRATEGY TIP

Catch blaze runts off guard by storming into battle with close-combat backup, such as cobblestone golems and zombies.

PORTAL GUARD

The piglin portals are key to their deadly advances, so the Horde of the Bastion assign their unique and ultra-tough melee battlers to defend them. Portal Guards are ultra-tough and will fight hoof and tusk to keep the portals safe. Their punishing chain-mace arms can clear you and your allies in one swing!

STRATEGY TIP

If you've cleared the rest of a base of threats, then ranged attacks will give you time to slowly wear portal guards down. However, if you're in a hurry and have golems to spare – advanced direct them to the portal to distract and weaken the guards.

WARBOAR

Unique to the Horde of the Hunt, you're unlikely to see warboars on their own as they prefer to roam in packs. They'll appear almost motionless and uninterested in you until you engage them. Once you do, they'll begin a charge attack – a fast melee move that will damage anything in its path.

STRATEGY TIP

If you see warboars initiate their charge attack, be ready to jump clear and counter with a swing of your sword. In Horde of the Hunt bases, try to locate the piglin pits with a snout on their banner. Destroy these to stop any more from being created.

SEEKER

Found in the Horde of the Hunt and Horde of the Spore, Seekers will stop at nothing to destroy you. You'll hear their distinctive cry as they rush to attack. They carry explosives that detonate as soon as they're close to you – taking everyone down!

STRATEGY TIP

You might not notice seekers until they're running towards you, giving you just a few seconds to react. Avoid them by quickly dodging out of their way, or destroy them using a group of projectile units.

LAVA LAUNCHER

This ancient-looking beast is unique to the Horde of the Spore. It will track you down and launch explosive blocks at your location. Their explosive range is so large that they can cause you damage from quite a distance. If you hear incoming projectiles ... run anyway!

STRATEGY TIP

Lava launchers are slow moving but quick to fire. Ranged attacks leave you exposed, so send some grindstone golems charging in!

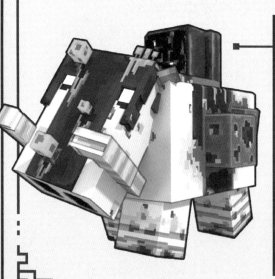

50

SPORE MEDIC

These specialist piglins patrol the battlefield, providing aid for their fellow soldiers. Their expert equipment spreads Nether spores to make the air breathable for piglins and heal wounded units.

BRUTE

The Horde of the Bastion's elite units, brutes are big, bad and built tough. Do not be fooled by their cumbersome ways, their whirlwind, spinning-blade attack will smash allied golems to bits before you even know they're in danger.

⊕ STRATEGY TIP ⊕

With dual blades and stone-crunching power, it's best to stay clear of brutes. Try placing upgraded arrow towers and scatter towers to fight might against might and take them down.

PIGLIN BUILDER

It's hard to accept, but piglin builders are adept engineers. Their powerful structures are very effective at polluting the Overworld. If you don't destroy them early, they'll build an impenetrable (and lethal) fortress.

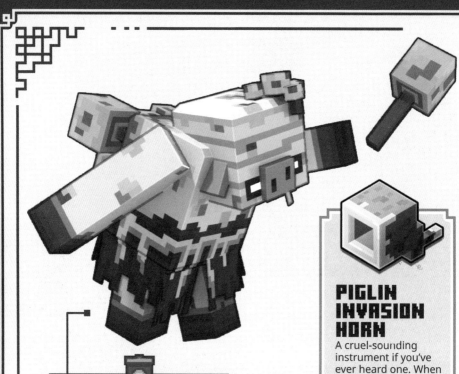

PIGLIN INVASION HORN

A cruel-sounding instrument if you've ever heard one. When blown, it signals piglin troops are moving, sending shivers across the Overworld. But don't back down – check your allies and be on high alert.

SPOREBACK

Sporebacks are the Horde of the Spore's crowd-control units. They specialise in ranged attacks, launching spore grenades that deliver a powerful knockback to you and your allies. This can damage your health and slow you down.

STRATEGY TIP

Direct your skeletons to aim and fire at these noxious nuisances. If your allies are overwhelmed, then fight them at their own game by placing a scatter tower upgraded with a spyglass overlook.

A well-balanced defence can make all the difference. Mix up your building strategy to defend against the different piglins.

PIGMADILLO

You don't become the Horde of the Hunt's elite unit without being seriously sinister. Pigmadillos are armoured monsters who will transform into wrecking balls that will bowl through you and your structures with devastating effectiveness. Keep them out!

STRATEGY TIP

Due to their armoured shells, pigmadillos are very tough to defeat. Use grindstone golems to stun them, then arrow towers and projectile units to wear them down.

PIGLIN INVASIONS

A hero's life can change from one day to the next. You might find yourself defending a desperate village one moment, and then storming an impossibly large base the next. On these pages, we will try to prepare you for every type of invasion.

VILLAGE INVASION

The villages of the Overworld weren't built to survive the force of the piglins. With their determination and strength in numbers, piglins will attack villages and imprison their innocent inhabitants – and then get to work on destroying the village fountain. Once you defeat a certain number of piglins, their remaining troops will retreat and plan another attempt with a mightier army. If you're too late, they will occupy the village and cause unthinkable damage.

PIGLIN OUTPOSTS

Outposts are a stain on the landscape of the Overworld. Varying in size, they can appear anywhere and their influence on the land cannot be underestimated. Their main purpose is to spread Nether spores across the Overworld, corrupting the air with spores and making the conditions perfect for piglins to start building bases.

Time is of the essence when the piglins attack. They grow stronger with each passing minute, so try to get to them as soon as possible.

PIGLIN BASES

If an outpost isn't cleared, it will soon cause the atmosphere to be toxic enough for piglins to expand their territory. This is when they will start building bases, complete with stronger piglin units and defensive structures, such as blaze rod towers. At their centre, a powerful portal gives them a direct connection to the Nether – destroy this and the base will be rendered useless.

SMALL BASES

Small bases are packed with barracks and short-range defensive structures. Although some are easy to access, others are protected by perimeter walls and will take work to get inside. If you struggle to make it to the central portal, try clearing out the surrounding units and structures to find a path.

LARGE BASES

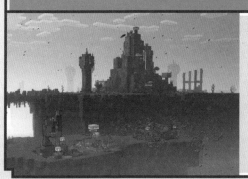

Large bases can often be fortified mega structures positioned atop steep cliffs. They are extremely difficult to access, but if you do make it inside, the piglins will throw everything they have at you with never-ending waves of resistance. If you make it as far as the portal, it will likely be protected by serious force.

ALLIES

Your journey as a hero will be dark and difficult, but shining through the darkness are the relationships you will build along the way. Some allies will be unexpected, but as news of your heroism spreads, mobs will gather to witness your might and join you for the fight.

GOLEMS

Golems are small mobs originally created by the Hosts, and now led by you. You can build spawners on the battlefield and spawn golems whenever you need them ... as long as you have the required resources.

PLANK GOLEM

This golem is a reliable defender of the Overworld. It will open fire and shower arrows on any nearby enemies, or you can direct it to structures where it will weaken them before you send in other mobs.

STRATEGY TIP

You can't place towers directly on netherrack, so plank golems are your solution for ranged attacks. They aren't the strongest, but a group of them provide serious power.

COBBLESTONE GOLEM

Spawned from simple stone, the cobblestone golem is as tough as old boots. Their melee attacks really pack a punch and a group of them have so much combined strength, they are a great method of taking down piglin structures.

STRATEGY TIP

Cobblestone golems are capable of destroying portals. If you clear a path for them, a large group can have the combined power to destroy entire bases.

MOSSY GOLEM

These friendly little golems might be gentle in nature, but they are very useful on the battlefield. They carry the waters of the Well of Fate and can use this to heal you and your allies during battles. If your health points have taken a hit, make sure you're close to a mossy golem.

✦ STRATEGY TIP ✦

When you're deep inside large bases, leaving the battlefield to replenish your health isn't an easy option. Rally some mossy golems so they can heal you as you go!

GRINDSTONE GOLEM

Call the cavalry and bowl over your enemies! Grindstone golems are fast-charging disruptors that will roll into groups of piglin units and leave them stunned. They are particularly useful when large groups of enemies appear from their piglin pits and need taking care of fast.

✦ STRATEGY TIP ✦

Thanks to their speed and determination, you can deploy grindstone golems to take down ranged piglin units – while you remain at a safe distance.

MEET THE MOBS

While you will discover mobs that you have never encountered before, there are others that look very familiar. Their behaviour, however, is not as you'd expect. They might be shy, but when the piglin invasion threatens their home, they will prove themselves to be valuable allies.

STRONGER TOGETHER

As news of your courage spreads, you will start to gain a reputation as a trustworthy hero. Slowly but surely, mobs will gather to witness your heroics. Keep this up and they may even decide to fight alongside you!

CREEPER

Creepers are the first mob to notice your heroic action in the Overworld. Their creeper homestead can be found in the dry barrens of the badlands biome. Protect it from a piglin invasion and this reclusive mob will become your ally – unlocking a lute melody to spawn them.

STRATEGY TIP

Keep creepers out of general combat because they don't often survive the melee. Reserve them for powerful and explosive attacks on structures and powerful foes.

Use the Battle View function to direct mobs to perform a task or demolish dangerous piglin structures, such as arrow towers.

ZOMBIE

There's no mistaking the moans and groans of this undead mob. If you discover some huts nestled deep in the jungle, then you can bet some zombies will be close by. You're wondering how they can come out in sunlight, right? Check out the shade under those hats!

✦ STRATEGY TIP ✦

Zombies may move slowly, but they're surprisingly strong. Use them for close combat and watch as they swing their arms and deliver powerful melee attacks.

SKELETON

They might be shy and quirky, but skeletons are a noble mob who will become a valuable addition to your army. If you find yourself in the tundra and discover a fierce skull base rising from the ice, then you're sure to find some skeletons gathered nearby.

✦ STRATEGY TIP ✦

For a mob with such shaky bones, skeletons have an expert aim. Use their ranged attacks to weaken piglin hordes and structures from a safe distance.

THE FIRSTS

The Hosts have been friends with the Firsts since the earliest days of the Overworld. These mighty golems used their unique powers to help make the lands. Now you will find them in deep slumber, and when you build the Wake the Firsts upgrade, you'll be able to make them your allies.

FIRST OF STONE

The First of Stone is one of the strongest allies you can call on. Much like the smaller cobblestone golem, the First of Stone is a master of melee and will make light work of smaller piglin units. However, its key attack is being able to launch boulders over long distances.

STRATEGY TIP

The First of Stone packs one of the hardest punches in the game. While it can send piglins flying, it can also launch rocks in ranged attacks that make light work of piglin structures. It also avoids taking damage, making it a super ally in battle.

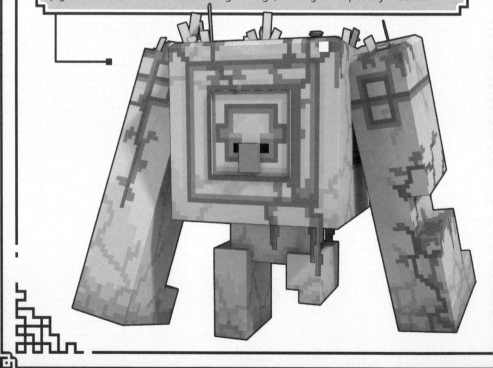

FIRST OF DIORITE

The Flame of Creation burning brightly at its fiery core enables the First of Diorite to spawn allies to fight alongside you. Even when your built spawners are far away, or have been destroyed, the First of Diorite will spawn new units that are ready to join your fight.

STRATEGY TIP

Taking on bases, such as the towering pillars of the Horde of the Spore, involves dangerous journeys. The First of Diorite will help rebuild your lost units as you go.

FIRST OF BRICK

First of Brick has always been a protector of the Hosts, the mobs of Overworld – and now you. As the Hosts built the mob homesteads, it used its shields to shelter the skeletons, zombies and creepers until their homes were ready. Now, it can use its shields to protect you when you need it the most.

STRATEGY TIP

If you're battling the Horde of the Bastion, who prefer ranged tactics such as lava launchers, the First of Brick offers much needed mobile shields for you and your allies.

FIRST OF OAK

The First of Oak has a close connection with the history of the flora of the Overworld and longs to protect the land. Its chest houses a powerful cannon that can be used to launch booming ranged attacks against piglin units and structures.

STRATEGY TIP

The firepower that the First of Oak brings will help break up any piglin tactics. It is useful in all battles, from village defence to destroying piglin barracks. Use the direct function to position it where you need it most.

ANIMALS

As you travel across the Overworld and witness all the different biomes, you will come across many other animals wandering the outskirts of villages or in the vast wildnerness. While most are passive beings, you might spot that some have attitude towards the piglins.

WOLF
You will often see wolves in packs, that will attack any piglins that get too close.

RABBIT
These critters enjoy the sunny plains and hopping across the shallow slopes around villages.

OCELOT
Prowling through the Overworld's jungles, ocelots are often found near to redstone ore.

CHICKEN
This passive mob is mostly seen enjoying the grassy biomes in peace and quiet.

PIG
This passive mob can be found enjoying one of the Overworld's many mud puddles.

FOX
If you see a flash of orange fur, you could be in the presence of a friendly fox.

TURTLE
As you cross waterways, you may notice an orange shell bobbing along, minding its own business.

LLAMA
The llama may look unassuming, but if a piglin so much as approaches one, it will start spitting in their direction!

BADGER
This new passive mob is elusive, but it is happy trundling around the Overworld's biomes.

WARRIORS

If you manage to counter the piglin invasion for long enough, you may discover you have a new ally that wants to join your fight. The Warrior is a brave brawler that could turn the battle in your favour.

INSPIRED BY A HERO

The more villages you defend and repair, the more word will travel of your heroics. Before too long, villagers will decide to follow your lead and will choose to stand up and start fighting. They are a powerfull ally.

WARRIOR

On first sight, you might mistake Warriors for the villagers you have been protecting throughout your campaign so far, but they are quite different. Warriors have watched your techniques and started to master the ways of war – and now they're up for the fight.

STRATEGY TIP

Warriors will spawn in villages, which is where you can gather them as your allies. Before you take on any piglin bosses, fast travel to unoccupied villages to increase your army of Warriors, ready for the battle ahead.

BOSS BATTLES

If you survive long enough to face a final fight with the Great Hog, Warriors will spawn on the outskirts of the action, so you can replenish your allies as you battle.

A Warrior's axe is a powerful tool. Swung with the heart of a hero, it is one of the most powerful melee techniques ever seen.

This mighty mob works well in a team with skeletons for their ranged attacks, and moss golems for healing support.

Warriors are one of the quickest allies available to you. Can you use their speed to your advantage?

PVP LEGENDS

If you're playing in PvP mode, you can spawn Warriors by building a Warrior Hut. This will let you call on the heroism of Warriors whenever you choose, but be warned: they have a high cost, so make sure you have lots of resources available!

GAME TACTICS

Now you have explored the Overworld and met the creatures which call it home, you need to know more about how you can help them. In this section, we'll show you how to build structures, command your allies and take the battle to the piglins.

FINDING YOUR WAY

Making your way across the land can be a daunting trial. You will travel long distances, encounter myriad foes and your heroic efforts will feel stretched to breaking point. Knowing how to navigate and prioritise your moves will be the difference between success and failure.

FAST TRAVEL

The quickest way to travel is by using the fast travel feature. Using your map, you can instantly teleport to any village fountain you have previously discovered, or back to the Well of Fate. You could also build a wellhouse that can be used for travel. Simply open your map, hover over a village or wellhouse and press the corresponding key to fast travel.

WAYPOINTS

It's easy to take a wrong turn and find yourself lost, especially in the dense jungles and snowy tundra. By opening your map and clicking where you want to navigate to, you can place a waypoint marker. This will remain as an icon on your compass, ensuring you always travel in the correct direction.

COMPASS

Running along the top of your screen is your compass. As well as showing the direction of any waypoints you've placed, it will guide you to the Well of Fate and villages, and alert you to nearby piglin bases. Occasionally a question mark will appear on your compass – follow it and you could come across a secret discovery.

Travelling long distance can take up valuable time. The fastest mount at your disposal is the regal tiger, which is perfect for racing across the Overworld. If you're up in the jagged peaks, the big beak is a powerful glider that can cross large distances without touching the ground.

USING MOUNTS

If you know you are going to explore a particular landscape, your choice of mount can save you lots of time and extra work. Climbing the jagged peaks on the regal tiger does not come recommended!

HORSE

The best all-rounder, it can cross all types of terrain with comfort, even if it takes a while. Perfect for tackling piglin outposts.

BRILLIANT BEETLE

This bug can scale mountains with ease and speed across water. Great for larger bases.

BIG BEAK

A good jumper, this feathered friend can glide for long distances and is a great choice for reaching any higher bases.

REGAL TIGER

This is the fastest mount on four paws, but is a slower climber. Best used to race to the rescue of villages in need.

SUMMONING GOLEMS

Every type of golem is crafted from the very land you are fighting to protect, so it should be no surprise that they are the first allies you encounter. Knowing how to summon these little powerhouses will be key to your early battles.

BUILDING SPAWNERS

Building spawners is a simple task that uses minimal resources. Firstly, choose the type of golem you want to spawn. Once your allays have built it, summon as many of each golem as you are permitted.

SPAWNING

You can spawn an army of one kind of golem, or a mixture to suit your tactics. Each spawn uses resources, depending on which mob you choose, so keep an eye on your gathered supplies.

RECALLING UNITS

During the course of a long journey or devastating battle, your golems can find themselves separated from you. You can recall them at any new or existing spawners, and bring them back to fight alongside you.

The losses of a difficult battle can sometimes see your golems outnumbered and overwhelmed. Upgrade at the Well of Fate and you can summon greater numbers!

COMMANDING ALLIES

Charging into even a small battle can end in great losses without the right tactics. By mastering the simple techniques to command your followers, you can take on the piglins efficiently and effectively.

BASIC COMMANDS

BANNER VIEW

By keeping your banner view button pressed, you can observe the action from an elevated angle. You can use this to direct your allies to key battle areas, or select mob types, such as creepers, to send on precision missions.

RALLY

Rallying is a way of telling mobs to follow you. This instant command will work on any friendly mob that's close to you, and they will follow you into battle or to a specific location until you hold the rally button down to make them stop.

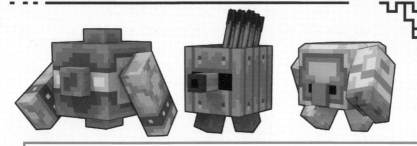

DIRECT

Directing is a simple but effective way of telling mobs which direction to travel. Tapping this command will make your hero raise the Banner of Courage and send any rallied allies whichever way you and your mount are facing.

FOCUS ATTACK

You can also command your allies to charge and attack a specific target. You can send a solo unit or as many as you choose, and they won't be distracted until they reach the location. They won't even stop to engage aggressive piglins.

CHARGE!

Send your allies charging into the action with this command. You can send one, two or all of your rallied mobs racing towards tyrannical piglin units or structures to engage in a fierce fight until none are left standing.

TYPE SELECT

The wisest heroes will soon learn that some mobs will be better suited to specific jobs or types of combat. Using this command will open a menu that enables you to quickly choose a specific ally or group of allies for any task.

BUILDING STRUCTURES

As the piglin invasion gathers pace and spreads across the Overworld, you will find it harder to help everyone that needs it. By building structures, you can provide valuable defensive help and also increase the strength and effectiveness of your own attacks.

WALLS

Walls are a simple but effective structure that can be used as your first line of defence against early invasions.

BUILDING

As long as you have gathered enough wood to build with, walls are one of the quickest ways of slowing down the damage piglins will cause to villages. Choose a starting point and then extend the wall where you'd like it to be built, creating a protective perimeter.

LINKING WALLS

If you are building sections of a wall at different times, you can join together existing walls to create a stronger defence. You can even place walls inside or outside an existing wall to add extra layers of protection.

REMOVING WALLS

You can remove sections of wall, one at a time, if you want to make changes. Simply stand close to it and interact when prompted and you can remove single block beams. This is useful if you wish to extend a perimeter wall or add space for other structures, such as gates or arrow towers.

DID YOU KNOW?

Building a masonry hut near wooden structures will permanently transform them into stone and make it harder for piglins to break them down.

RAMPS

Using ramps is a great way to gain access to new locations, especially if your journey takes you across valleys or between two of the Overworld's tallest peaks, or even to gain access to something much more dangerous, such as a base.

BUILDING RAMPS

Select ramp and then choose a starting spot. Holding down the place button, you can drag the hologram to your target location, then click again to place your ramp. Useful for crossing lava moats or climbing steep cliffs.

REMOVING RAMPS

If your bridge is connecting two areas you will visit again, it might be useful to leave it in position. If it was used only to access a now-destroyed piglin base, you can remove it and claim back the resources you used to build it. Stand next to it and interact to remove it and your build allays will take it down.

BLUE IS BEST

When placing any structure, the blue placement hologram will turn red if you are unable to build where you want. This could be down to not having enough materials or because you can't build on surfaces covered with nasty netherrack.

STRUCTURES

The ability to build structures is vital to your success. You can't be everywhere at once, and your structures will work for you by keeping villages protected while you're not around.

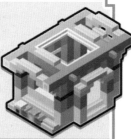

BUILDING STRUCTURES

Every structure in the Overworld requires its own amount of free space to be built. Once selected, a blueprint of the structure will appear on the ground. If there is an obstacle preventing you from building, simply drag it around until you find a suitable location.

STRUCTURE RANGE

Most structures have a range of effectiveness, outside of which they offer little use to you or your allies. For example, a carpenter's hut needs to be built close to village fountains or it won't repair them. Counter-offensive towers, such as an arrow tower, will only fire once piglins have entered into their range.

REMOVING STRUCTURES

If you no longer need a structure to perform a task or if you wish to move it elsewhere, you can task your building allays with dismantling it. They'll operate quickly and will return valuable materials to your inventory.

You can add an explosive kickback to projectiles, such as those fired from arrow towers, by building a kaboomery nearby.

TOWERS

There are three mysterious towers that you may discover across the Overworld. They were crafted long ago by the Hosts and their powers were long forgotten. If you prove yourself worthy, you may be able to unleash them ...

BLAST TOWER

The blast tower stores energy from lightning, and uses its power to deliver a devastating electrical shock to piglins that stray within its range.

FROST TOWER

This ice-cold tower fires frosty cubes at approaching piglins that will freeze and slow them down for a limited time, allowing you to counterattack.

STUN TOWER

If you want to cause chaos and confusion for your enemies, the stun tower delivers a booming sonic attack – leaving them stupefied and disorientated.

BUILDING TOWERS

To use these powerful towers, you first need to unlock the Collect Power Towers improvement. Each tower has a core resource that you will need to use to construct them. If piglins destroy a tower, you won't be able to repair it, so protect them with defensive walls and arrow towers.

REMOVING TOWERS

As you can only use each collected tower once, you might choose to remove them and build them again elsewhere – where you need their power the most.

PIGLIN STRUCTURES

From the smallest outposts to the biggest bases, every piglin structure is designed to tighten the piglins' hold on the Overworld and to further their ultimate aim to take it for themselves. Knowing their strengths and weaknesses is key to stopping them.

PIGLIN GATES

Gates look like the best place to enter a base, but they are guarded by scores of piglin units who will be waiting for you if you do make it in. Don't be fooled by an open gate – it will close if you stray too close.

PIGLIN WALLS

Bases are sometimes surrounded by huge walls, which your allies will struggle to climb over. While you can use the brilliant beetle to scale them, you need to find a way to let your allies through.

PIGLIN PITS

These are used to deploy piglin units within bases. There are three types, and each delivers different classes of piglins. Each pit has a banner, which shows you what will spawn there.

The explosive power of a creeper is useful throughout battles, but it is particularly strong if you need to clear an entrance to a base for you and your allies.

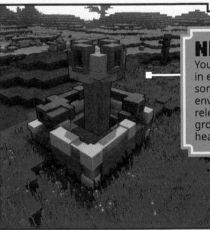

NETHER SPREADERS

You will find these peculiar structures in every type of piglin base and some outposts. They transform the environment into a toxic wasteland, releasing a poison that will cover the ground in netherrack and damage your health levels.

TERROR HORN

Be warned. The terror horn emits a fear that can cause any of your units within its range to become consumed by panic.

GOLD EXTRACTOR

Piglins are obsessed with gold, so they use these to mine gold from below the Overworld's surface. Destroy a base and you'll be able to gather any gold they have.

PIGLIN LAUNCHER

This long-range tower acts as a mobile barracks by launching barrels filled with piglins. Larger bases will launch higher classes of piglins, and these structures can even send terrifying warboars flying through the air.

TOWERS

Standing above the shadows of piglin bases, towers are their greatest form of defence. Ignoring them will cause significant damage to you and your allies. Approach with extreme caution and a plan for tackling them.

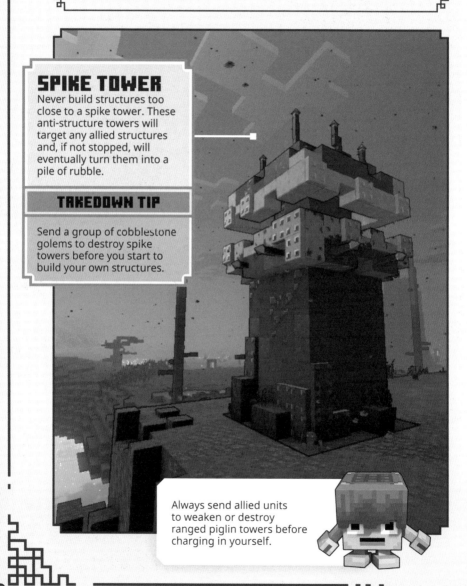

SPIKE TOWER

Never build structures too close to a spike tower. These anti-structure towers will target any allied structures and, if not stopped, will eventually turn them into a pile of rubble.

TAKEDOWN TIP

Send a group of cobblestone golems to destroy spike towers before you start to build your own structures.

Always send allied units to weaken or destroy ranged piglin towers before charging in yourself.

BLAZE ROD TOWER

After piglins themselves, blaze rod towers are the biggest threat to your survival. Stray within range of one and it will fire frequent blaze rods your way with devastating accuracy. They should be one of your first targets in every base.

TAKEDOWN TIP

Gather any skeleton allies you have and command them to open fire. In larger bases, destroy them from a safe distance using the power of a redstone launcher.

SPORE TOWER

This anti-unit tower was designed with the sole purpose of knocking back approaching enemies with a powerful blast of toxic spores. It's so ferocious that golems can't even get close before being knocked away.

TAKEDOWN TIP

With their limited range, it is best to attack spore towers using ranged attackers such as skeletons, or tougher allies such as the Firsts.

LAVA COILS

If you see lava coils in bases, then you've got a tough task ahead. They provide a layer of magma to piglin portals, which acts as a force field. You won't be able to damage these portals until they are gone.

LAVA MOAT OUTPOST

The toughest part of tackling a lava moat outpost is actually reaching it. You'll need perfectly placed ramps to cross the bubbling lava moats. Prepare to take down the outpost walls with cobblestone golems and ranged allies.

PORTAL

At the centre of every piglin base stands a portal. These imposing structures are a direct link to the Nether and are used to transport armies of piglins to join their invasion of the Overworld. Once a portal is destroyed, the whole base will fall.

FOCUS TARGET

In smaller bases it might be possible to bypass other defences and send your troops directly to the portal. This can save time, but could cause larger losses.

HEAVILY GUARDED

As the most important part of a base, portals are defended by countless units, and more could teleport through at any moment.

CLEAR A PATH

To gain safe access to a portal, you will need to clear the structures that surround it. Use the direct command to send your allies straight to things that can cause you harm, such as towers and piglin pits.

INVASION TACTICS

The piglins are extremely calculated and they will do everything in their power to stretch your efforts and catch you off guard. To beat the enemy, you must first understand how they operate and what you need to consider to match their tactics.

PIGLIN INVASIONS

You will mostly encounter piglins through the night, but will also see smaller, less ferocious groups roaming the Overworld during the day. When the sun rises, they occupy themselves with the careful planning of their nightly targets.

NIGHTLY ATTACKS

While some piglins are busy building bases, many are deployed to attack the Overworld's villages. They prefer to operate under the cover of darkness, so will always invade as the sun goes down. You can discover which villages are being targeted by opening your map. If any village on your map has a red target over it, it will be attacked at nightfall.

NEW BASES CREATED

When their outposts have polluted the land and poisoned the air, piglins will start to build bases. An existing base that is left to stand will soon be marked with a banner on your map. If you don't manage to destroy this base by nightfall, a new small base will be built on the corrupted land surrounding it.

PIGLIN BASE UPGRADED

There is never a moment wasted by the piglins, and any bases left alone will soon be upgraded into enormous bastions of terror. Upgraded bases are protected by more units and can be surrounded by giant walls that reach far into the sky – and make access much more difficult. If, on your map, a base is marked with a banner, it will upgrade to a bigger size at the end of the day.

Always remember to use your map for more than your own exploration of the Overworld. It's the easiest way to identify piglins' movements and ghastly ambitions.

VILLAGE DEFENCE IDEAS

Those pesky piglins can have bases everywhere, but if they can't destroy village fountains, then they won't achieve their goals. These simple methods will help you defend villages even if you and your allies aren't able to be there.

TRIPLE WALLS

Walls are simple and strong but will only keep piglins out for so long. Gather as much wood as you can and build triple walls. Three walls set close together will provide a perimeter that is much harder to break through and make the piglins a sitting target for your defensive structures.

TOWERS

Turrets just inside your village walls will open fire on any piglins that try to break through. Using upgrades will make them more durable and increase their firing range, so consider a battle drum or kaboomery (remind yourself of their uses on page 41).

DEFENSIVE THINKING

Using specific structures in certain positions can lead to effective results. Placing freeze traps in front of towers will slow down enemies and protect structures. Masonry huts placed inside villages will turn any walls and towers in their range into stone, making them much harder for piglins to destroy.

Your structures will only last so long before piglins break down their effectiveness. Always return to villages to ensure they are safe and make repairs.

BATTLING THE HORDES

At first glimpse, the three piglin hordes will seem just as greedy and brutal as each other. While they are equally barbarous, they are all unique and their behaviours and bases pose many different challenges.

HORDE OF THE BASTION

LONG RANGE
This horde's long-range mentality makes it difficult to reach their base without suffering serious damage and great losses. Try planting decoy structures or posting allies away from you. That could distract their attention.

BREAKING THROUGH
Always scout the entire perimeter of bases for areas that aren't as fortified with structures. You can make your own path inside by using creepers, the First of Stone or a redstone launcher to force your way through.

INCREASED SPAWNING
When their portals take damage, their piglin pits will begin to spawn defensive units at a vastly increased rate. Try to destroy these structures early to decrease your chances of being overrun by units later in the fight.

RAPID REPAIRS
This horde will act fast to repair any damages you cause to its base. This could result in you becoming trapped inside its walls and being forced into close-quarters combat, unable to escape to regain health points. Be prepared!

HORDE OF THE HUNT

HUGE ARMIES

No other horde spawns armies as large as the Horde of the Hunt. Destroy their piglin pits to avoid being overwhelmed by their sheer numbers.

STRATEGIC BASES

The Horde of the Hunt prefer designing their bases with deadly defences in close proximity to their portals. Make sure you remove their Nether spreaders and blaze rod towers before you stray too close to their portals.

QUICK TO REACT

If there is one thing this horde dislikes, it is when you build your own defences. If you build structures anywhere near their bases, they will explode with rage and hunt you down. They will also attack any structures you build to defend villages.

HAZARDS

As if working your way through their bases wasn't hard enough, they are covered in extra hazards. Reinforced bone walls make navigation difficult and piglins are unharmed by the slow grow brambles that will cause damage to you and your allies.

HORDE OF THE SPORE

GAINING ACCESS
Horde of the Spore bases are all found on top of huge pillars with treacherous valleys in between. It's vital to build ramps to cross platforms and advance through the levels of each base – so always gather as much wood as you can carry before you begin.

SECRET PATHS
Every base is a navigational nightmare and finding your way in can be puzzling as well as extremely perilous. Keep your eyes peeled for hidden routes in, as the terrain surrounding the towers sometimes offers sneaky access paths.

PROTECTOR TOWERS
This horde loves nothing more than spreading their evil and will attack trespassers with wave after wave of lava launcher attacks. Try using protector towers to shoot them out of the sky before they can rain down on you and your forces.

BANNER VIEW
The complexity of these bases make them incredibly difficult to get to, and the Spore's piglins will make it even harder. They will throw everything they have into distracting you, so use banner view to maintain a good overview of the action.

PIGLIN BOSSES

There will come a time when the piglin powers will grow tired of you interfering and will send in their big bosses. When this happens, you'll face a fight unlike anything you've encountered before. Defeating them will lead you in one direction ... to an epic meeting with the Great Hog themself.

THE UNBREAKABLE

By plunging their arm into the terrain, they cause geysers to violently erupt!

The boss of the Horde of the Bastion, the Unbreakable will punish anything that gets in their way. When you spoil their plans one too many times, you will find them lingering menacingly near the portal of a new base – just waiting to unleash their mighty cannon arm against you.

If they line up a target, their cannon arm can send a stream of deadly fire in the direction of you and your allies.

STRATEGY

The Unbreakable has the unique ability to use their own powers to manipulate the Overworld's natural features to cause unnatural damage. Try to keep a safe distance, so their fiery throngs can't hurt you. Using explosives will give you the best chance of inflicting critical damage, so consider a creeper army and scatter towers (with as many upgrades as you can afford).

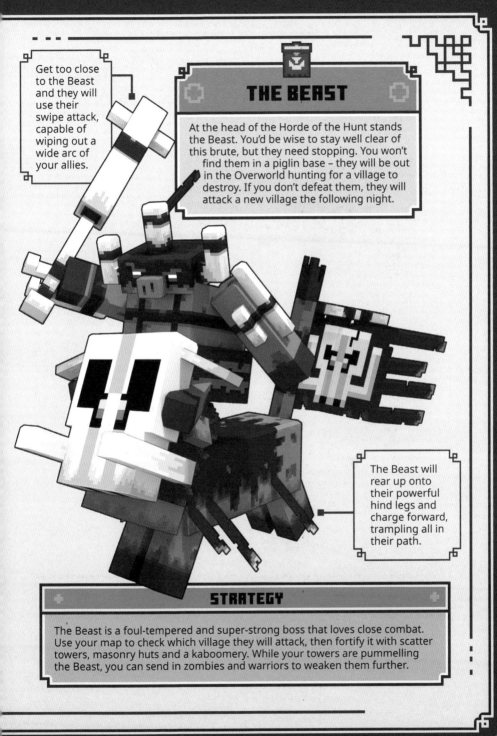

Get too close to the Beast and they will use their swipe attack, capable of wiping out a wide arc of your allies.

THE BEAST

At the head of the Horde of the Hunt stands the Beast. You'd be wise to stay well clear of this brute, but they need stopping. You won't find them in a piglin base – they will be out in the Overworld hunting for a village to destroy. If you don't defeat them, they will attack a new village the following night.

The Beast will rear up onto their powerful hind legs and charge forward, trampling all in their path.

STRATEGY

The Beast is a foul-tempered and super-strong boss that loves close combat. Use your map to check which village they will attack, then fortify it with scatter towers, masonry huts and a kaboomery. While your towers are pummelling the Beast, you can send in zombies and warriors to weaken them further.

Their back is covered in rapidly growing spots that explode to release damaging toxic spores.

THE DEVOURER

There is no mistaking which horde this putrid boss belongs to. Above the Horde of the Spore's infested bases, you will find the Devourer patrolling elevated platforms that are difficult to reach.

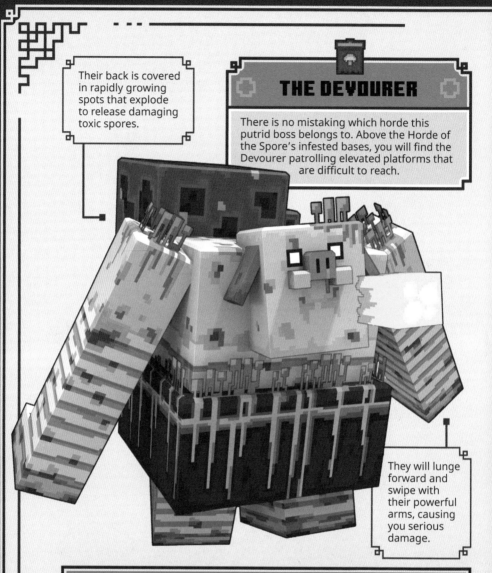

They will lunge forward and swipe with their powerful arms, causing you serious damage.

STRATEGY

The Devourer is hard to defeat due to their ability to jump great distances between platforms. Once you cause them enough damage, they will launch to a new location. Due to their poisonous features, your safest tactic is with ranged attacks, so the skills of skeletons, plank golems and towers are your best method of attack. Distract them with units or they will single you out.

THE GREAT HOG

Their axe and spear can be used to stun and swipe enemies, sending any nearby allied units flying.

By smashing their weapons into the ground, they send electricity to stun and damage their enemies!

If you can defeat the three horde bosses, you will come face to face with the Great Hog. Enraged that you have beaten their top commanders, they will embark on an all-or-nothing final attack. If successful, it will be devastating. It's time to put every alliance you've made and strategy you've learned to the ultimate test!

STRATEGY

The Great Hog is the biggest challenge any hero can face. With their burning rage, and their axe and spear, there are many ways they can cause critical damage to you and your allies. If you manage to break through the bases surrounding them, be prepared with spawned mobs, allies and repeated explosive tactics.

FINAL BATTLES

If you've made it as far as the boss battles, then you already deserve the title of hero, but your biggest challenge is about to begin. These tips will help take your tactics to the next level.

BE PREPARED

Once you enter a boss battle, the action will escalate at an alarming pace. Make sure you have the resources to build as much as you need. If you need more, fast travel to a village to gather its chest rewards. This is especially useful after the shared village chest upgrade.

CONSIDER YOUR APPROACH

Knowing what to expect from each boss will directly affect your chances of success. Watch how they move and observe how they react. Identify a weakness, then put together your own plan on how to use all your skills to defeat them.

HEALTH WATCH

Always keep an eye – or an ear – on your health. If it gets too low, you will hear a sound to alert you. If this happens, try to leave the danger zone immediately and allow your health bar to recover. You will lose less progress doing this than allowing yourself to perish. If you have a mossy golem nearby, run to it.

SPAWNERS NEARBY

Always place spawners near your battles. Certain allies are more powerful against particular bosses, so position the best-suited spawners where you can access them quickly. You never know when you'll need to replenish your army and start with a new approach.

DISTRACTION TECHNIQUES

Piglins are often distracted by your allied units or structures. Quickly placing an arrow tower, or positioning small groups of units in different locations, can take their attention away from you. Use this time to build structures, such as redstone launchers, or to direct different mobs to specific tasks that suit their strengths well.

BATTLE BAR

WHICH TACTICS ARE MOST EFFECTIVE AGAINST WHICH BOSSES?

THE UNBREAKBLE

CREEPERS	FIRST OF BRICK	MOSSY GOLEMS

THE BEAST

ZOMBIES	FIRST OF STONE	STONE GOLEMS

THE DEVOURER

SKELETONS	FIRST OF OAK	PLANK GOLEMS

THE GREAT HOG

CREEPERS	WARRIORS	STRUCTURES

GOODBYE

There you have it: Make friends, save the world. Seems simple, right? If only it were that easy. Now get out there and make your own legend.

The Overworld is counting on you!

- MOJANG STUDIOS